First Picture Dictionary
Animals

Primer diccionario ilustrado
Animales

Pig
Cerdo

Rabbit
Conejo

Butterfly
Mariposa

Fox
Zorro

Illustrated by Anna Ivanir

www.kidkiddos.com
Copyright ©2025 by KidKiddos Books Ltd.
support@kidkiddos.com

All rights reserved. No part of this book may be reproduced in any form or by any electronic or mechanical means, including information storage and retrieval systems, without written permission from the publisher, except in the case of a reviewer, who may quote brief passages embodied in critical articles or in a review.
First edition, 2025

Library and Archives Canada Cataloguing in Publication
First Picture Dictionary - Animals (English Spanish Bilingual edition)
ISBN: 978-1-83416-255-3 paperback
ISBN: 978-1-83416-256-0 hardcover
ISBN: 978-1-83416-254-6 eBook

Wild Animals
Animales salvajes

Lion
León

Tiger
Tigre

Giraffe
Jirafa

✦ *A giraffe is the tallest animal on land.*
✦ *Una jirafa es el animal terrestre más alto.*

Elephant
Elefante

Monkey
Mono

Wild Animals
Animales salvajes

Hippopotamus
Hipopótamo

Panda
Panda

Fox
Zorro

Rhino
Rinoceronte

Deer
Ciervo

Moose
Alce

Wolf
Lobo

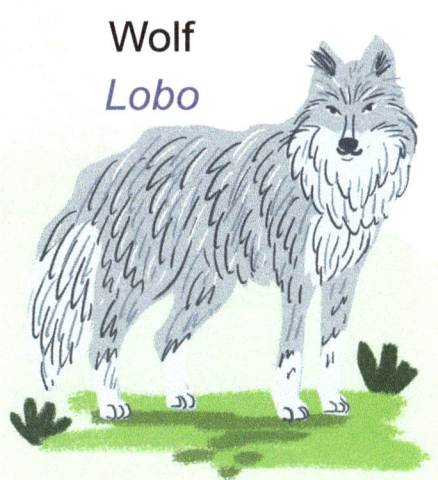

✦ A moose is a great swimmer and can dive underwater to eat plants!

✦ ¡Un alce es un gran nadador y puede bucear para comer plantas!

Squirrel
Ardilla

Koala
Koala

✦ A squirrel hides nuts for winter, but sometimes forgets where it put them!

✦ ¡Una ardilla esconde nueces para el invierno, pero a veces olvida dónde las puso!

Gorilla
Gorila

Pets
Mascotas

Canary
Canario

Guinea Pig
Cuy

✦ *A frog can breathe through its skin as well as its lungs!*
✦ *¡Una rana puede respirar por la piel y por los pulmones!*

Frog
Rana

Hamster
Hámster

Goldfish
Pez dorado

Dog
Perro

◆ *Some parrots can copy words and even laugh like a human!*
◆ *¡Algunos loros pueden copiar palabras e incluso reírse como los humanos!*

Cat
Gato

Parrot
Loro

Animals at the Farm
Animales de la granja

Cow
Vaca

Chicken
Gallina

Duck
Pato

Sheep
Oveja

Horse
Caballo

Mosquito
Mosquito

Dragonfly
Libélula

✦ *A dragonfly was one of the first insects on Earth, even before dinosaurs!*
✦ *¡Una libélula es uno de los insectos más antiguos de la Tierra, incluso anteriores a los dinosaurios!*

Bee
Abeja

Butterfly
Mariposa

Ladybug
Mariquita

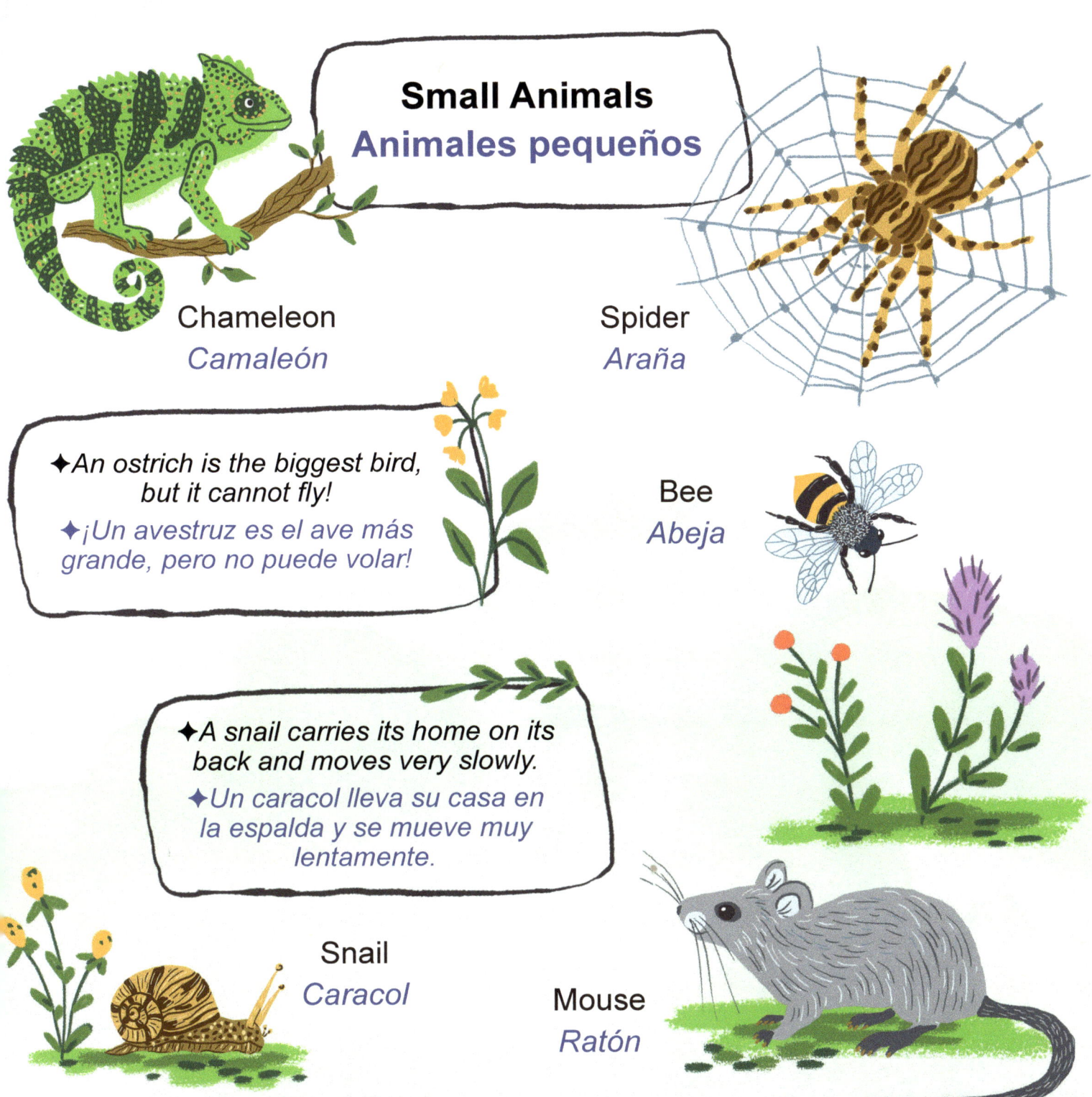

Quiet Animals
Animales silenciosos

Ladybug
Mariquita

Turtle
Tortuga

✦ A turtle can live both on land and in water.
✦ *Una tortuga puede vivir en la tierra y en el agua.*

Fish
Pez

Lizard
Lagartija

Owl
Búho

Bat
Murciélago

✦ A firefly glows at night to find other fireflies.
✦ Una luciérnaga brilla en la noche para encontrar otras luciérnagas.

✦ An owl hunts at night and uses its hearing to find food!
✦ Un búho caza de noche y usa el oído para encontrar su comida!

Raccoon
Mapache

Tarantula
Tarántula

Colorful Animals
Animales coloridos

A flamingo is pink
El flamenco es rosa

An owl is brown
El búho es marrón

A swan is white
El cisne es blanco

An octopus is purple
El pulpo es morado

A frog is green
La rana es verde

✦ A frog is green, so it can hide among the leaves.
✦ *Una rana es verde, entonces puede esconderse entre las hojas.*

Animals and Their Babies
Animales y sus crías

Cow and Calf
Vaca y Ternero

Cat and Kitten
Gato y Gatito

✦ *A chick talks to its mother even before it hatches.*
✦ *Un pollito habla con su mamá antes de nacer.*

Chicken and Chick
Gallina y Pollito

Dog and Puppy
Perro y Cachorro

Butterfly and Caterpillar
Mariposa y Oruga

Sheep and Lamb
Oveja y Cordero

Horse and Foal
Caballo y Potro

Pig and Piglet
Cerdo y Cerdito

Goat and Kid
Cabra y Cabrito

www.ingramcontent.com/pod-product-compliance
Lightning Source LLC
LaVergne TN
LVHW072003060526
838200LV00010B/268